BIRDS AND BEASTIES

BY SHEENA NELSON

Dedicated to the Kent wildlife trust for doing a sterling job keeping the garden of England safe.

INDEX

Robin----- Page 4
Hedgehog-----Page 6
Blackbird-----Page 8
Bumble bee-----Page 11
Sparrow-----Page 13
Ants-----Page 15
Starlings-----Page 16
Damselfly-----Page 18
Dragonfly-----Page 19
Canada geese-----Page 20
Bush crickets-----Page21
Blue tit-----Page 23
Great tit-----Page 24
Dung beetle-----Page 25
Wood pigeon-----Page 26
Collared dove-----Page 27
Butterflies-----Page 28
Sparrowhawk-----Page 34
Highland cow-----Page 35.

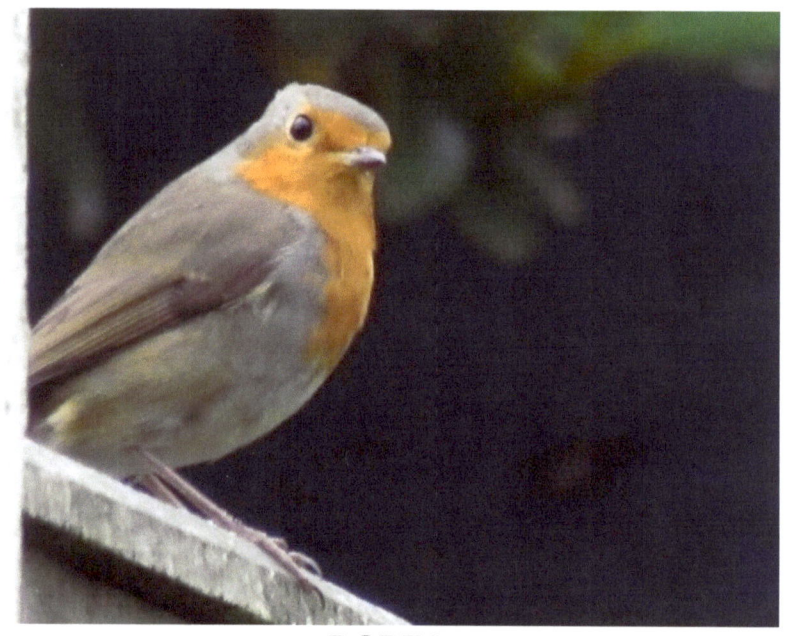

ROBIN

Robins aren't only here at Christmas time; they are here all year round.

They have a lovely song and like to sing a lot. The males sing to tell other Robins that he is there so they don't come into his territory.

Robins eat insects and fruit so if you have a garden get some mealworms or finely grated cheese and put them on the ground then wait and you might be lucky to see a Robin.

Robins can be quite tame so if you are quiet each time you see one it will get used to you then it will stay near when you go outside.

They lay 4-5 eggs which are bluish white with sandy red freckles. If you spot a nest in the bushes or anywhere else then look at it quietly but do not touch it otherwise the parent birds might leave the nest and the babies will die. Robins use their red breasts to show other robins so that other robins won't enter their territory. Robins like to have their own space and do not like sharing.
Female Robins are lighter and baby ones don't have a red breast at all.

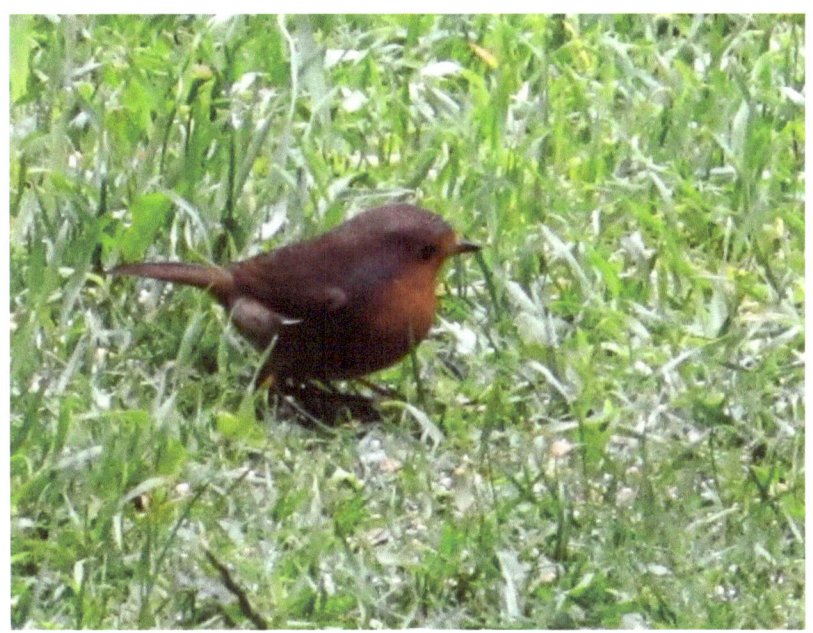

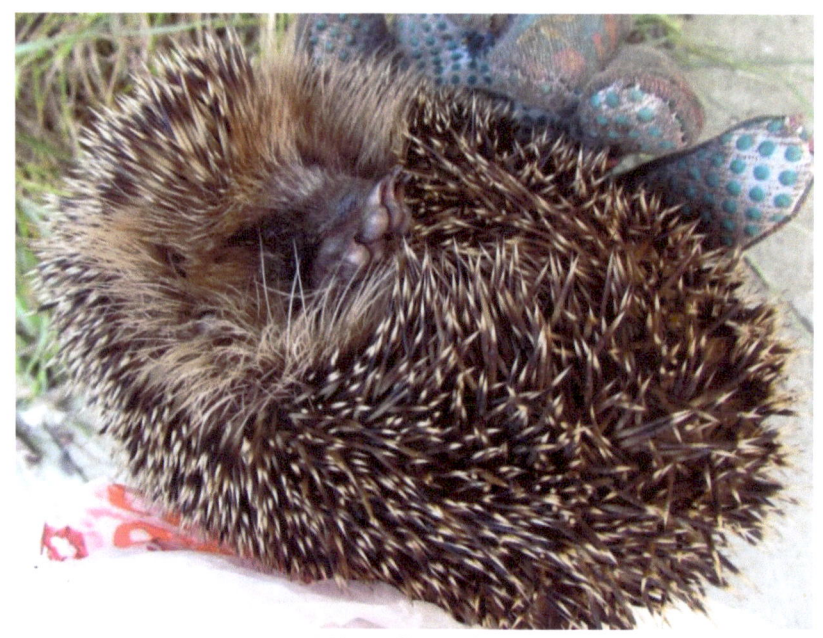

HEDGEHOG

Hedgehogs are very cute looking animals but they are actually very spikey. If you see one don't pick it up. Get an adult to do it with gloves on like in the picture.

The spines on a hedgehog can be 3cms long and are really sharp. When they are scared or being attacked they roll into a ball with their prickles sticking out so that they can't be eaten.

They like to go in the undergrowth and in gardens. You can entice them in your garden by building a hedgehog house. A wooden box with a lid and a hole in the front with leaves in or straw. Make sure there's a hole under the fence too.

Hedgehogs are very good for the garden as they eat slugs, snails and other bugs. You can put out cat or dog food for them.

Hedgehogs are getting quite rare so we need to look after them.

They are nocturnal which means they only come out at night to hunt for food but sometimes they can be seen in the day time.

Hedgehogs hibernate all winter in dry leaves and grass. They curl up and go to sleep all snuggly when it gets cold and wake up in the spring.

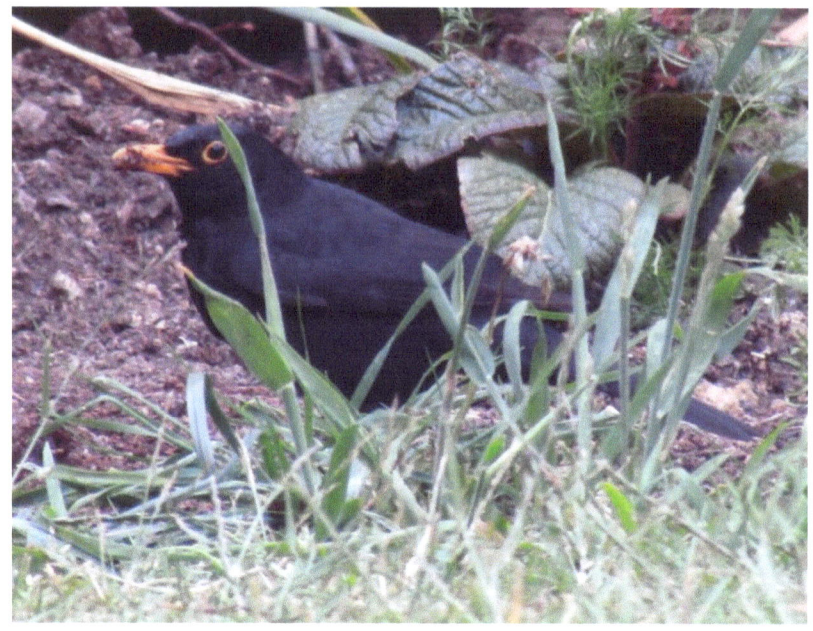

BLACKBIRD

Blackbirds are seen a lot in gardens. They have a beautiful song.
It's only the males that are black though. The females and babies are a mottled brown colour.
They feed mainly on worms.
They have 3-4 eggs in tough nests in the forks of branches.
The eggs are greenish blue with reddish brown marks.
Their orange beaks can be seen from a distance. They use their beaks to crack snail shells as do Thrushes. They eat snails if no worms are available.
Blackbirds are here all year round.
Put some mealworms or grated cheese out on the ground and see if they come.

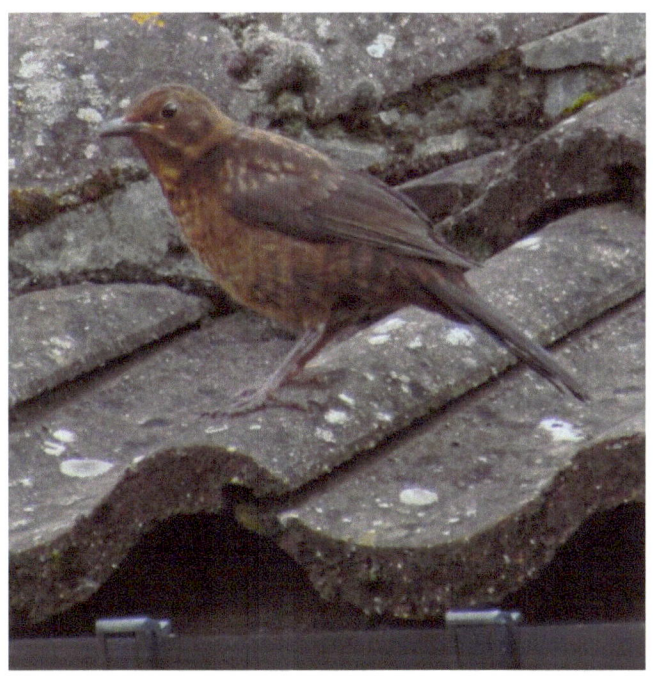

A baby Blackbird waiting for his food. See how he is brown and spotty so that he can hide in the undergrowth and not be seen. This is called being camouflaged.

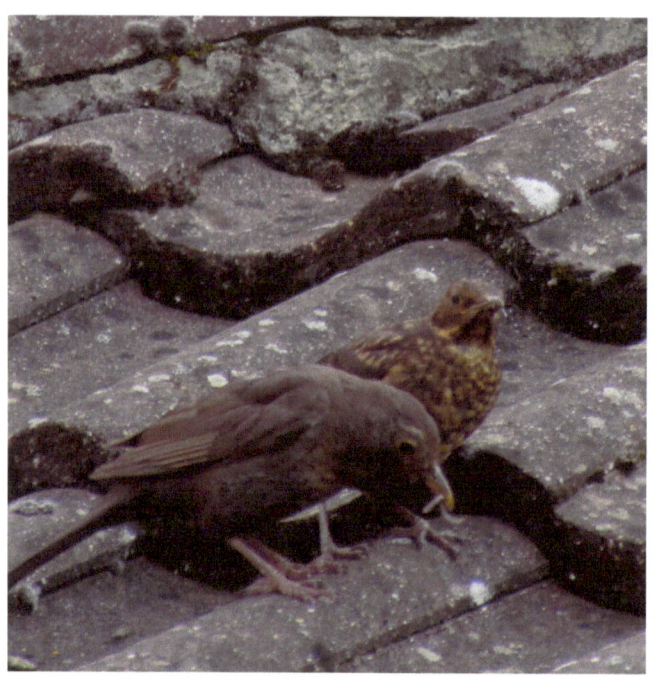

Mother and baby Blackbird.

The mother Blackbird has caught a worm to feed to the
baby who has not learnt to get his own food yet.
Soon he will learn to find his own food, learn to fly and
eventually get black feathers. The mother bird stays this
colour.

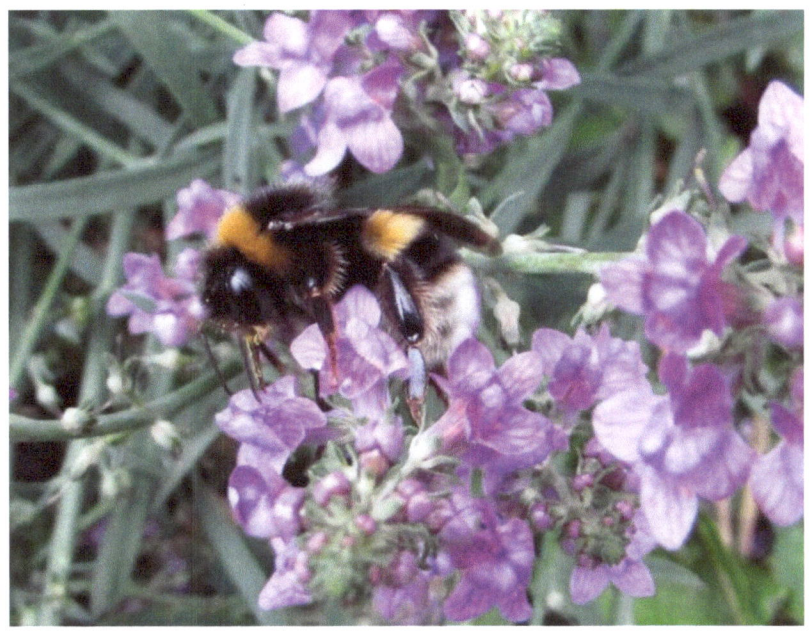

BUMBLE BEE

Bumble bees are cute looking furry beasts but they do sting so be careful. When they sting they die because they leave some of their body in the sting so will only attack things if they really have to.
Bumble bees live in nests of up to 400. Some nest under the ground and some in holes in trees and other things. There is always a queen bee who lays lots of eggs and worker bees look after them.
The queen only lives a year then another queen will grow up and hibernate through the winter then start another nest.

Bumble bees are finding it hard to find flowers so try and plant some nice flowers with lots of pollen like single roses and foxgloves. You can even plant some flowers in a pot on a windowsill outside if you don't have a garden, it all helps.

Bumble bees and honey bees help pollenate our food so we need them and they are lovely creatures and a joy to watch.

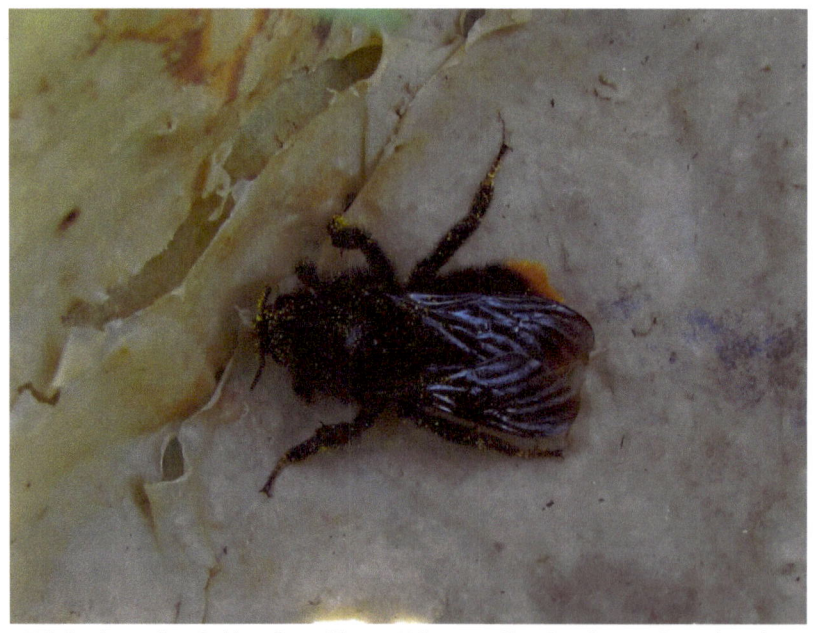

This bee is full of pollen. If you find a bee that looks sleepy you can revive it by putting some white sugar mixed with slightly warm water in a tiny bowl near it then watch it drink it and fly off.

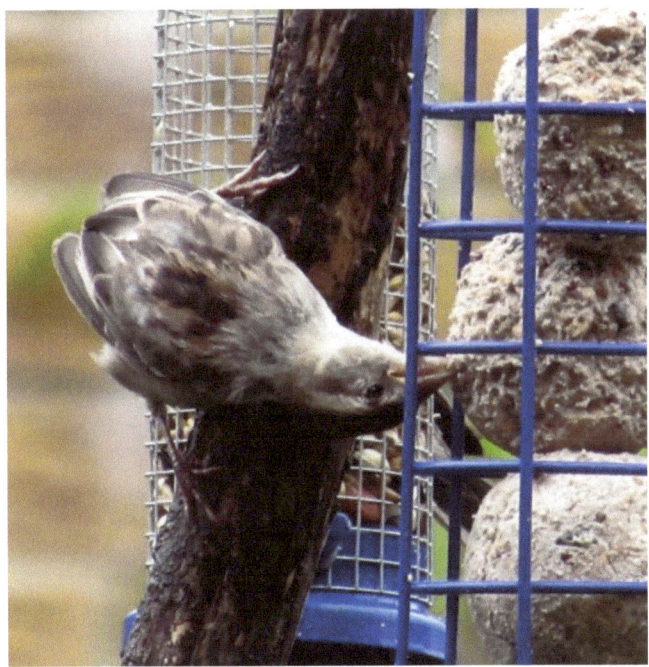

SPARROW

This little tree sparrow is trying a different way to get food
out of the fat ball hanger.

There are two different kinds of Sparrows that live here in
Britain, the tree sparrow and the house sparrow.

Tree sparrows are smaller than house sparrows and are
also lighter in colour.

They eat mainly seeds from the ground so put some bird
seed on the ground in your garden although as you can see
they will eat fat balls and some small insects.

They lay 3-6 eggs each time and they can lay up to 4 times
a summer.

They nest in cracks in walls or climbing plants. Some nest in holes in trees or they like to nest in nest boxes in gardens. Eggs are whitish speckled with brown.

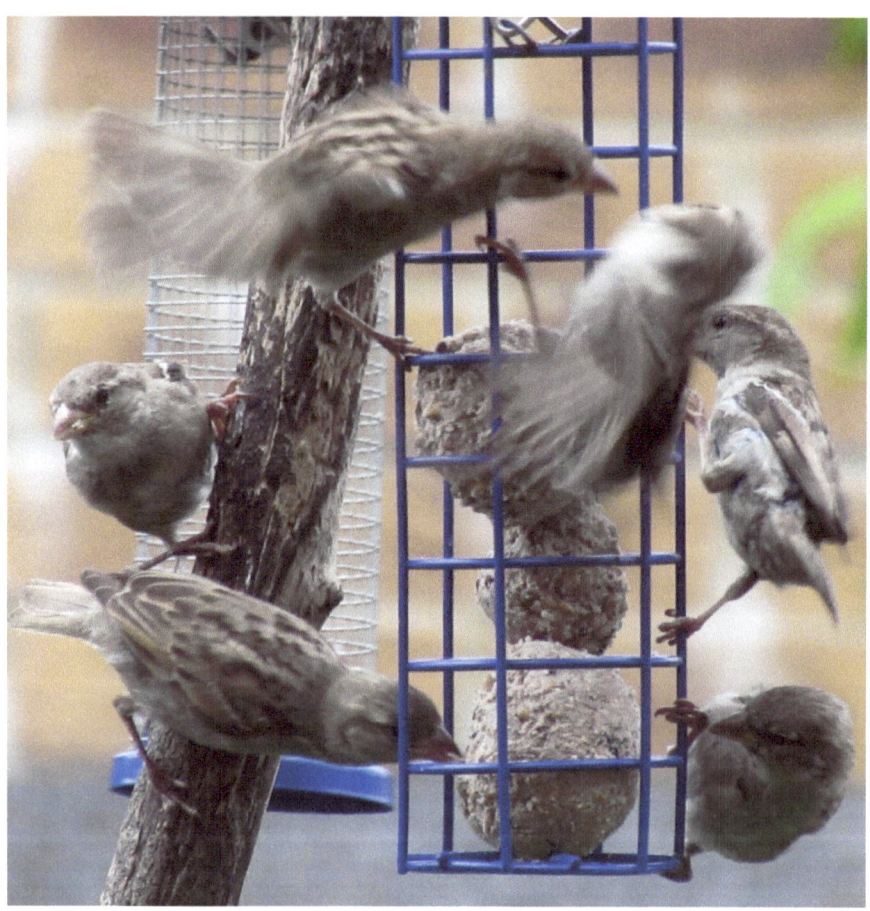

SPARROWS FEEDING

These house and tree sparrows are fighting over the fat balls, all wanting to eat at the same time.

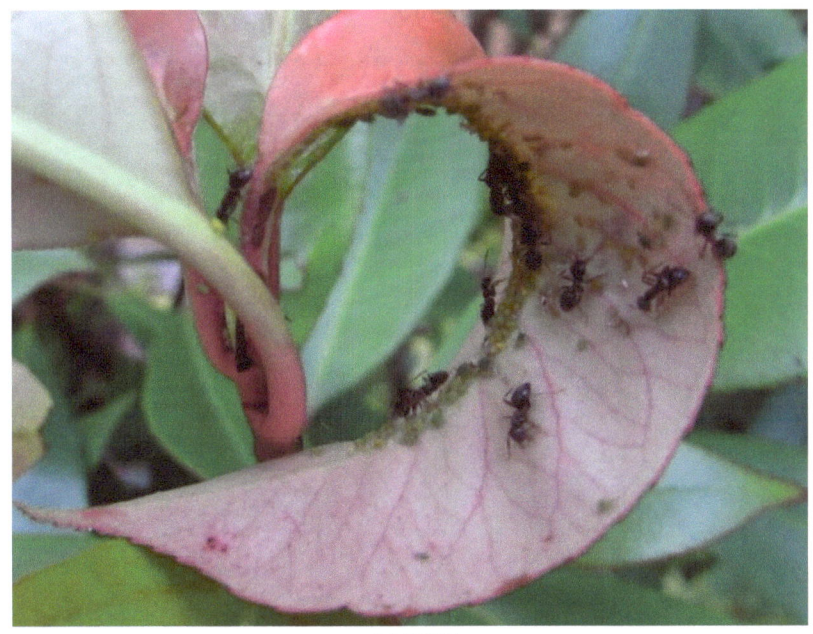

ANTS

Ants live under things like logs, bricks, paving slabs and
pots. Some species build mounds though or live in old
trees.
They live in a big colony with worker ants collecting food.
Black garden ants like in this picture like honeydew which
is secreted from aphids like greenfly. The ants farm the
aphids and tickle them to make the honeydew come out so
they can eat it or take it back to their nest for the larvae.
Ants are very interesting to watch. You can get ant farms
which are made of glass so that you can see the ants
burrowing.

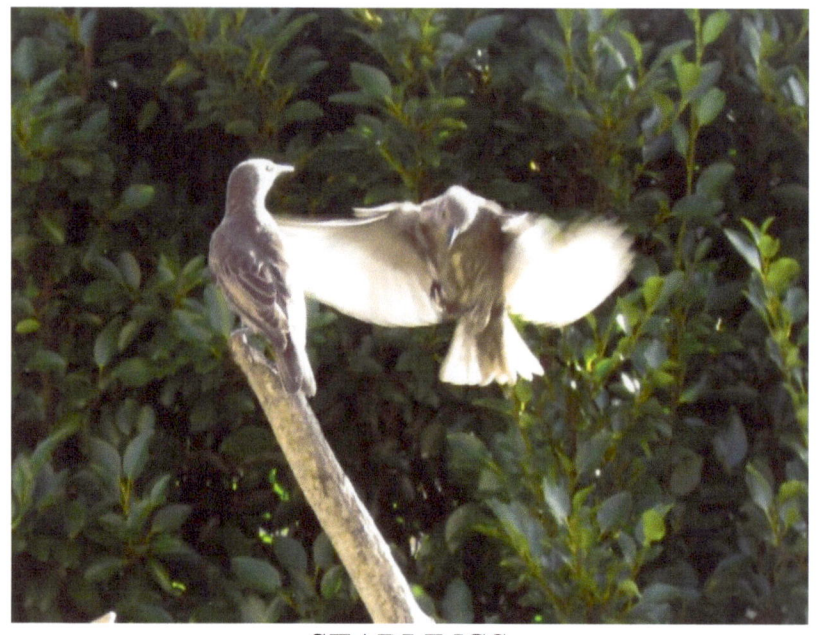

STARLINGS

Starlings like to flock together and can be very noisy especially when they argue and fight over food.

The male ones have blackish feathers spotted and look oily. They shine in the sun. The females and young ones are paler. You can see a young one on his way to growing up as he has spotty feathers coming through his pale ones.

Starlings gather together in their hundreds in the winter and fly around the sky making patterns before they go to bed. This is called a murmuration.

They lay 4-7 eggs which are pale blue.

Watch some starlings, they are very interesting birds and fun too.

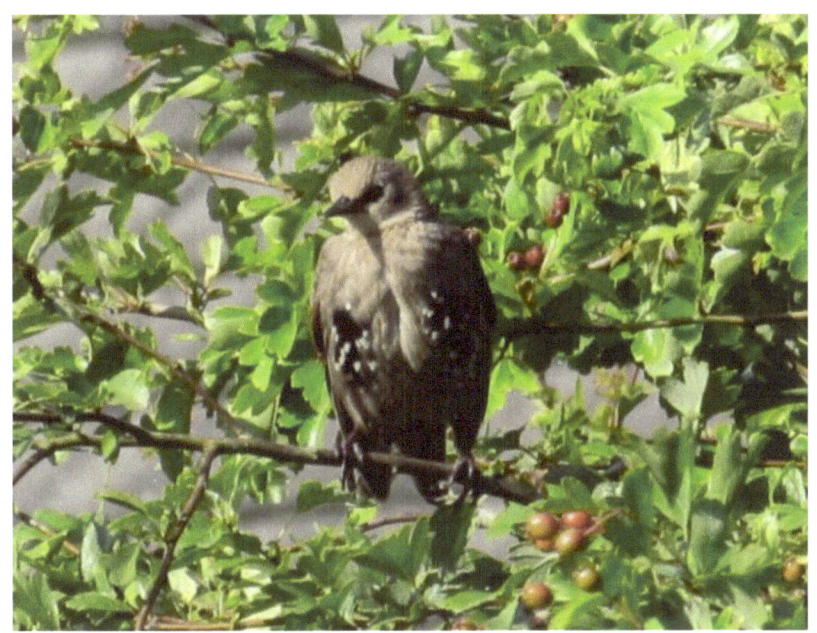

BABY STARLING

As you can see this is a baby Starling about a year old that
has begun to get his adult spotty feathers.
Look at their long tough beaks which are very good for
getting insects and seeds.

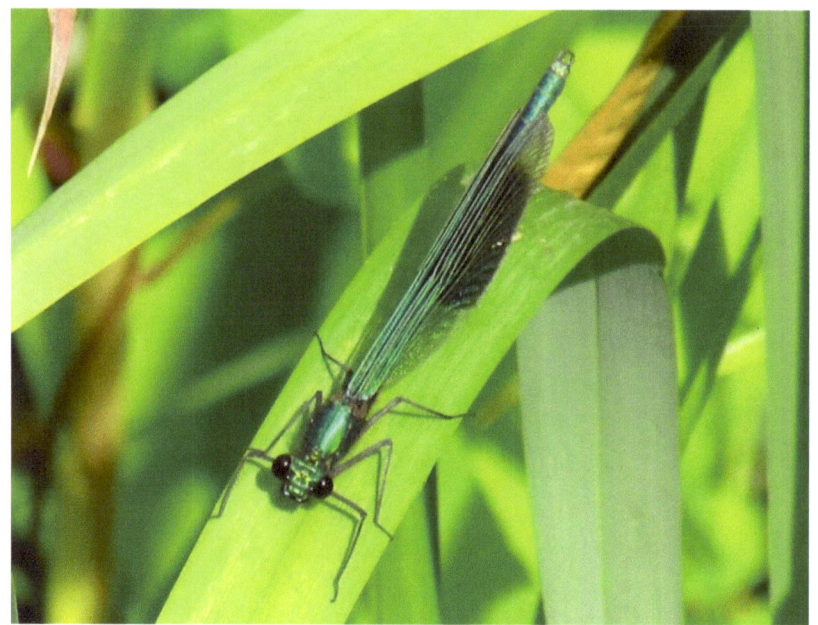

BROAD WINGED DAMSELFLY

This beautiful Damselfly can be seen flying and resting around water. This is a male one, the females are browner. The larvae live under the water for a long time eating tiny creatures until they are ready to change then they crawl up stalks. The skin dries and splits and a beautiful Damselfly appears, warms up then flies off.
These are smaller and thinner than Dragonflies. Also look for bright blue ones with black stripes.

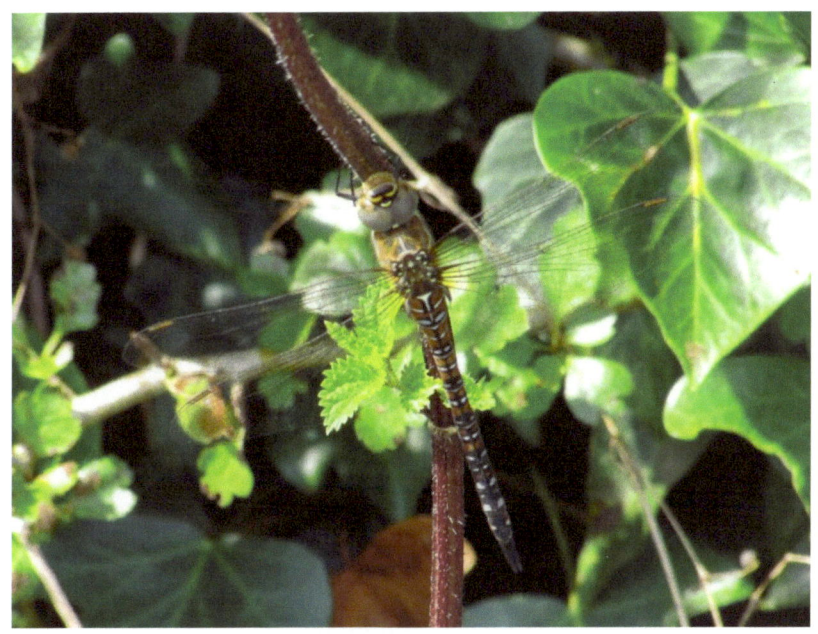

DRAGONFLY

As you can see Dragonflies are a lot larger than Damselflies. Their lifecycle is the same though.

Go down to a pond, lake or canal in the summer and sit still for a while and you should see a lot of these wonderful creatures flitting around catching gnats to eat or basking in the sun on a leaf or branch.

These are some of my favourite animals.

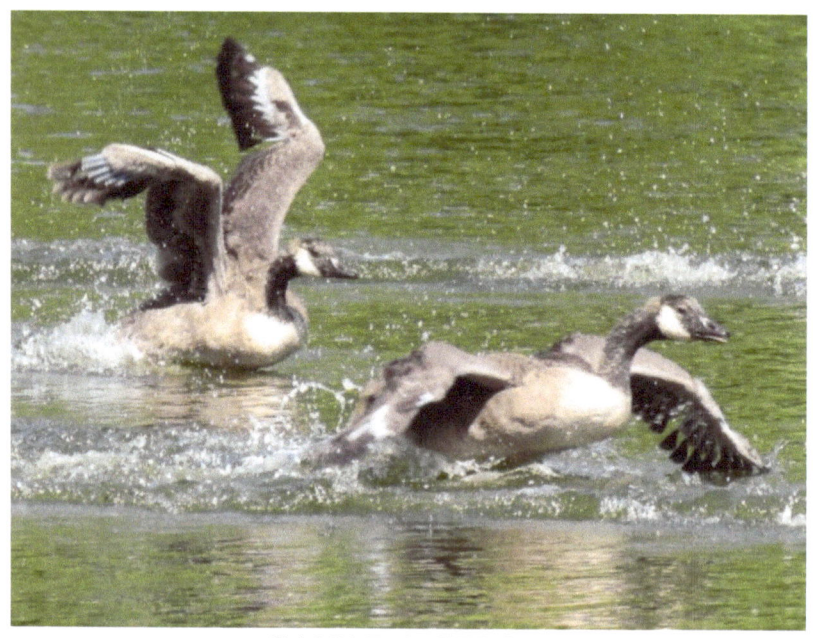

CANADA GEESE.

These strong large geese are taking off on a lake. Canada geese are not native to Britain as the name suggests they were brought over here from Canada to put on lakes.
They feed on grass and cereals, not bread. Bread is actually not good for swans ducks and geese. You can buy special duck food now from pet shops.
The geese make a nest on the ground usually on islands in lakes. They have 5-6 eggs which are creamy mottled brown.
Canada geese can live up to 25 years.
Go to a lake and watch their powerful flight and hear their honking noise.

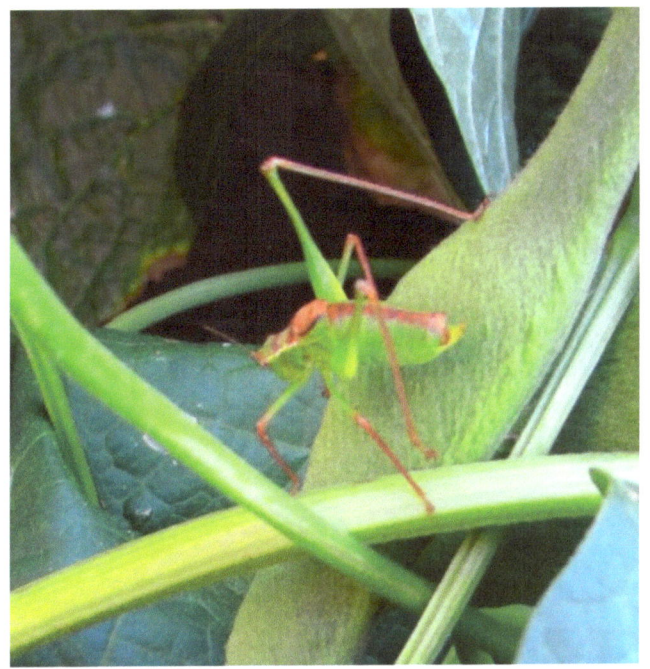

BUSH CRICKET.

This is a bush cricket not to be mistaken with a grasshopper or a ground cricket although similar these are bigger and are found mainly on bushes. This one is on a willow.
They have really long antennae and large back legs so they can jump a long way.
There are several different bush crickets, some are brown and some are bigger.
They feed on small insects.
Look carefully on leaves as they are camouflaged.

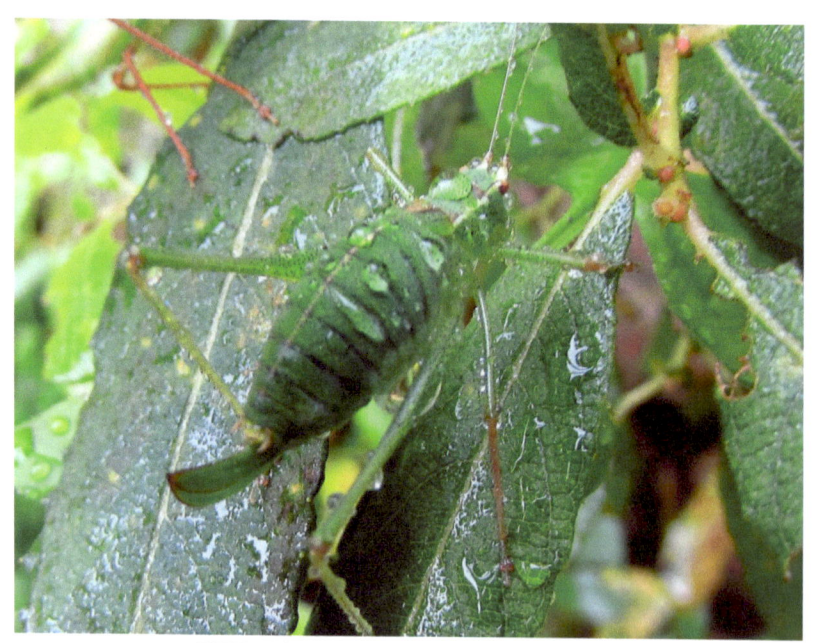

FEMALE BUSH CRICKET.

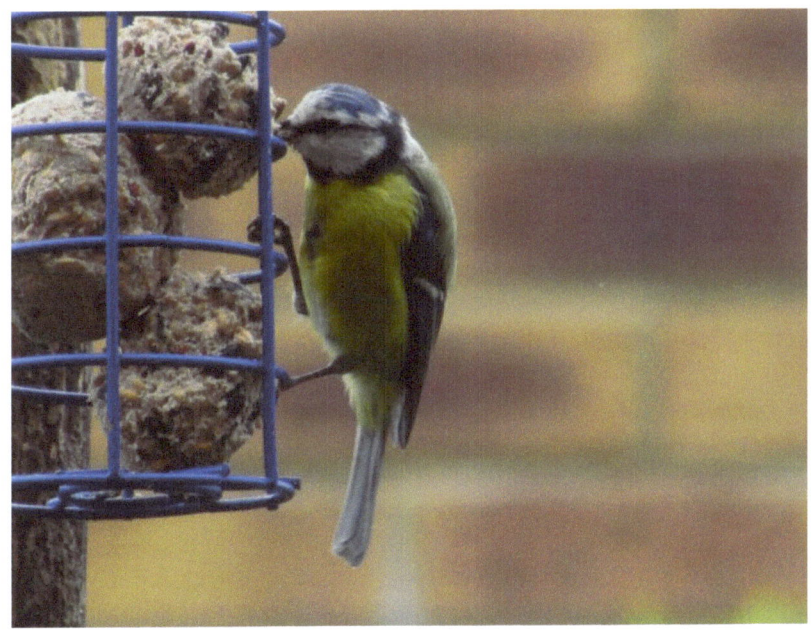

BLUE TIT

This is a little sweet Blue Tit. There are quite a few different Tits including, great tits, coal tits and long tailed tit.
Blue tits have a lot of babies so need a lot of food. 8-10 eggs, white with red brown spots are laid in a small comfortable nest built in holes or nest boxes.
They feed on insects and spiders and also eat seeds in the winter.
They are lively little birds and are fun to watch flying about with their bright blue head and wings.

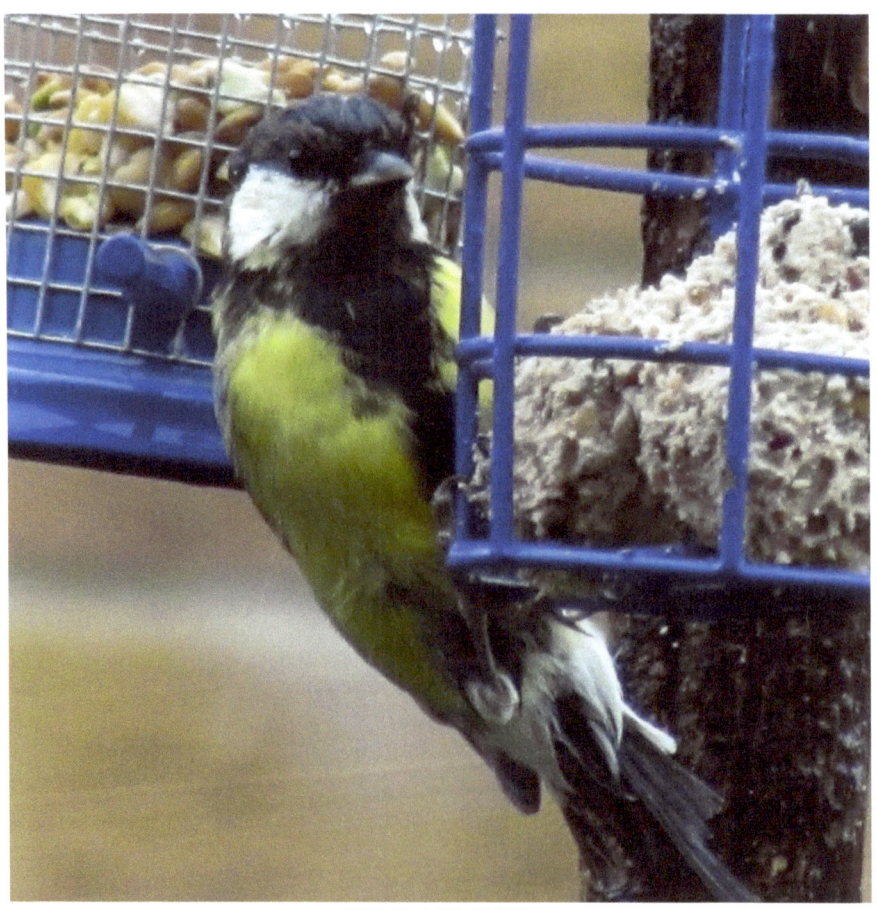

GREAT TIT.

The great tit is larger and darker than the blue tit but still
has a yellow tummy.

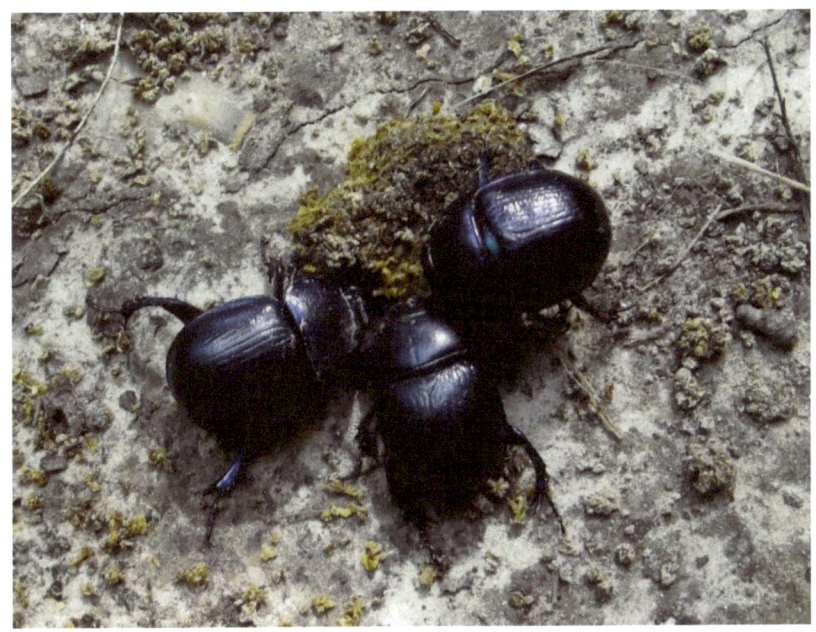

DOR OR DUNG BEETLES.

These handsome beasts are shiny black beetles that like poo. Yes not a nice thing to eat but they love it and feed it to their baby larvae which are in a little tunnel underground.

The beetles eat it or roll it along to their tunnels. They are very good to have around as they get rid of animal poo like cow pats and horse dung.

If you look closely you can see that they are shiny like oil on water.

When you are walking in the woods or fields be careful and look at the poo lying about and you could find a lovely dung beetle getting its dinner.

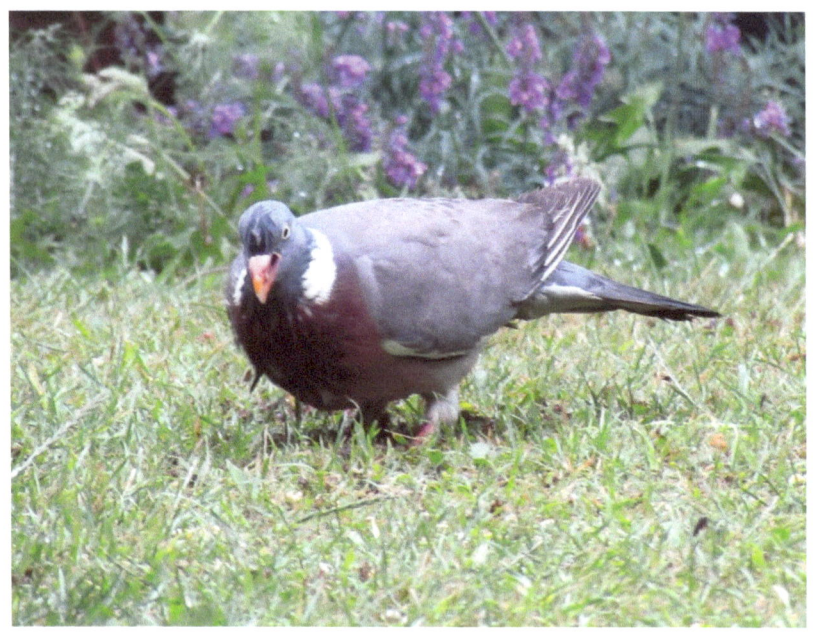

WOOD PIGEON

This is a wood pigeon. They are bigger than town pigeons or racing pigeons and live in the woods and fields.
They have a very distinct call.
They are also bigger than the collared dove which is a creamy colour with a dark collar.
They make nests in trees out of thin twigs and lay 2 eggs which are cream coloured, a bit like chicken eggs.
They eat buds, leaves, berries and fruit and bird seed from gardens.
They are very strong heavy looking birds, watch them strutting around or flying from tree to tree.

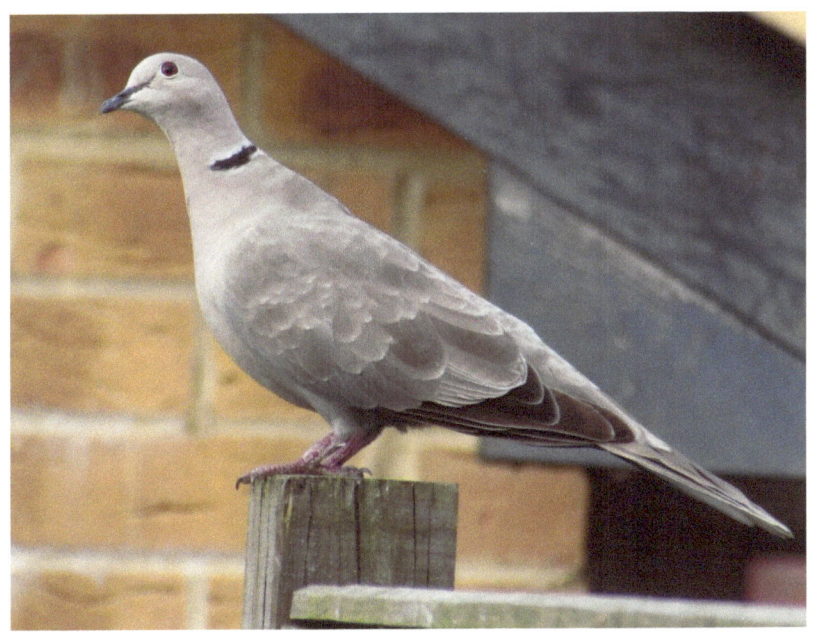

COLLARED DOVE

This is the collared Dove, as you can see it's smaller and lighter than the Wood Pigeon. They eat the same as wood Pigeons and have similar nests.

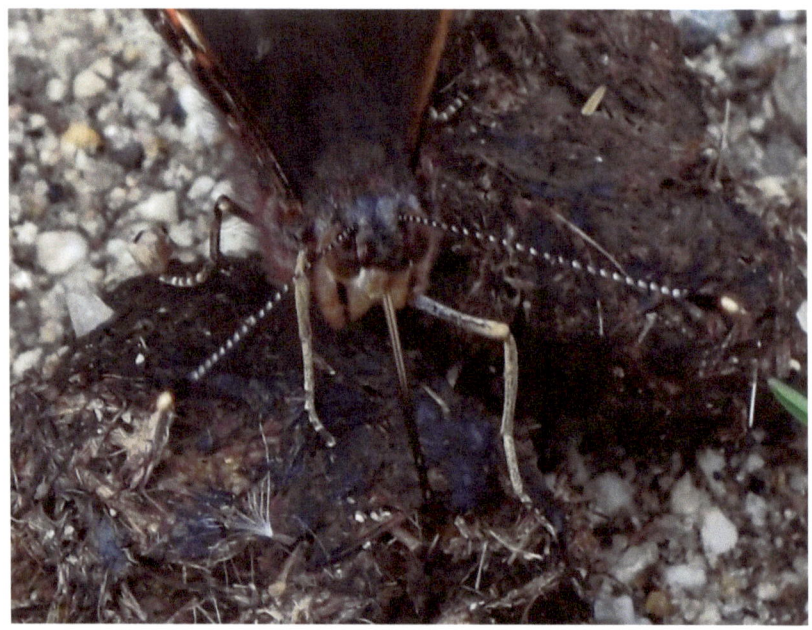

SMALL TORTOISHELL BUTTERFLY

This butterfly is sucking out the moisture and nutrients
from horse poo.
Usually they will be drinking nectar from flowers but need
other nutrients and water as well so can be found on poo or
mud as well.
They will often be seen in the house in the winter where
they hibernate until spring.
They lay eggs on stinging nettles.
There are many different kinds of butterfly so keep looking
and see how many you can count.
There is an annual butterfly count every year in July and
August which you can join in with. The butterfly
conservation society has all the info.

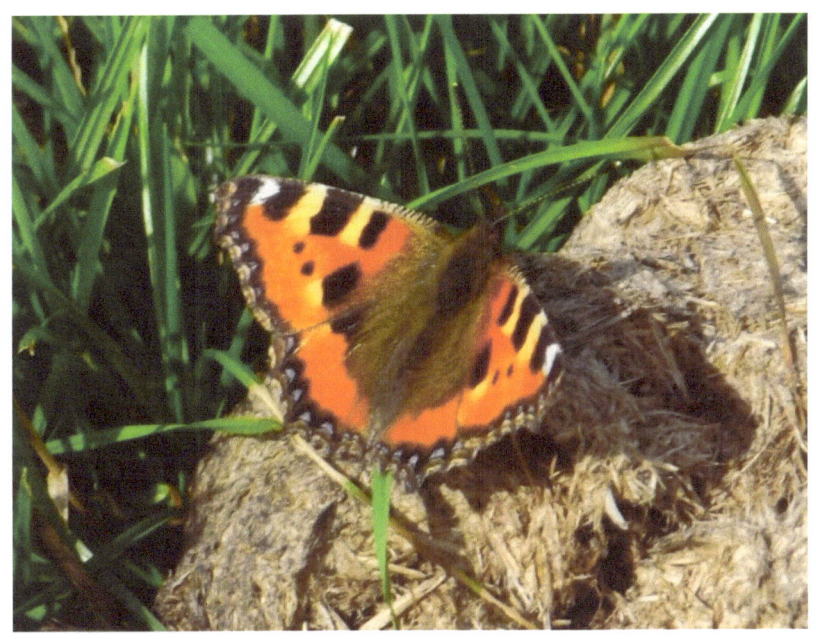

SMALL TORTOISHELL ON MANURE.

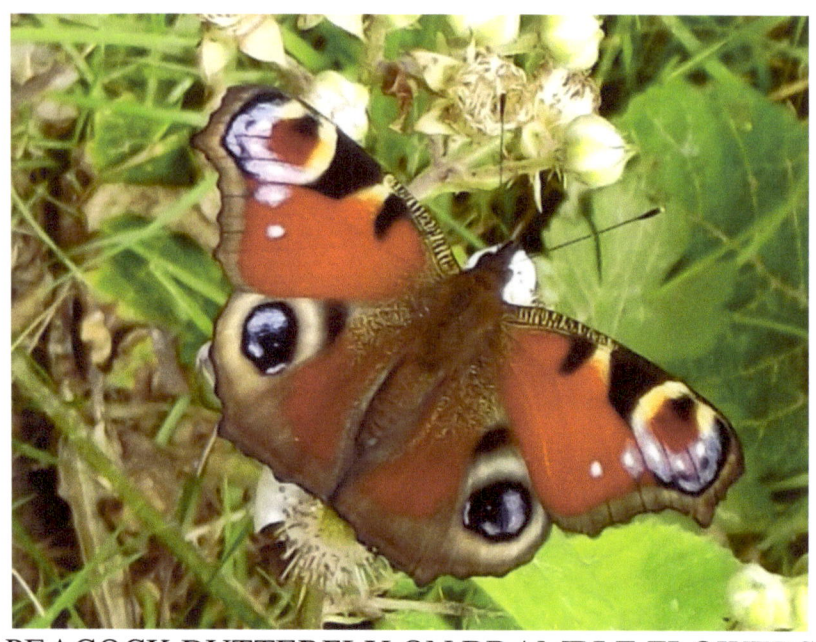

PEACOCK BUTTERFLY ON BRAMBLE FLOWERS
Some butterflies like this peacock have markings like eyes
and red warning markings to stop being eaten. Other
butterflies look just like leaves.
Also look out for caterpillars on nettles and in bushes, also
on flowers like nasturtium or ragwort.

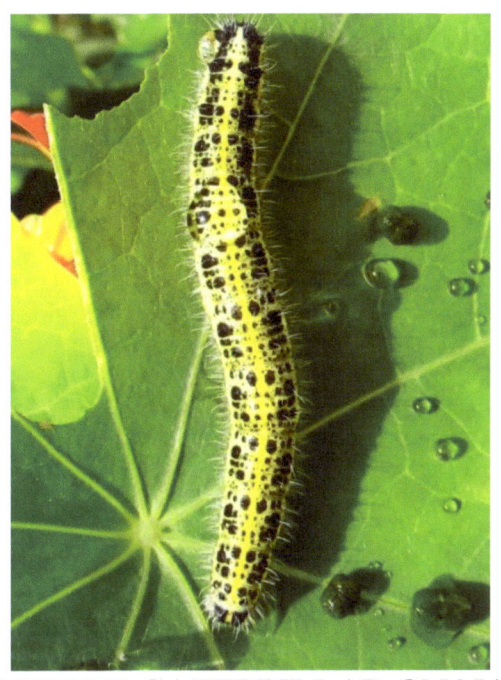

CABBAGE WHITE CATERPILLAR ON NASTUTIUM LEAF.

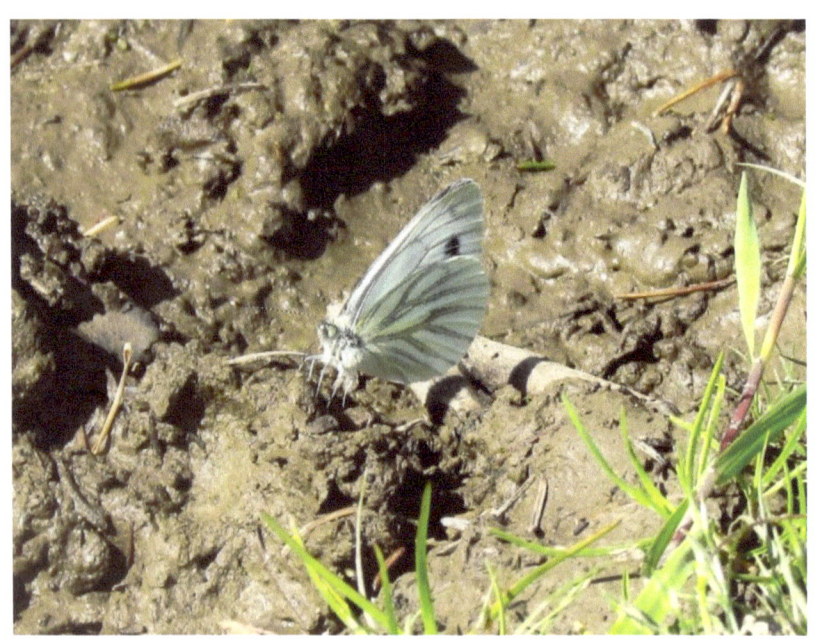

GREEN VEINED BUTTERFLY ON MUD

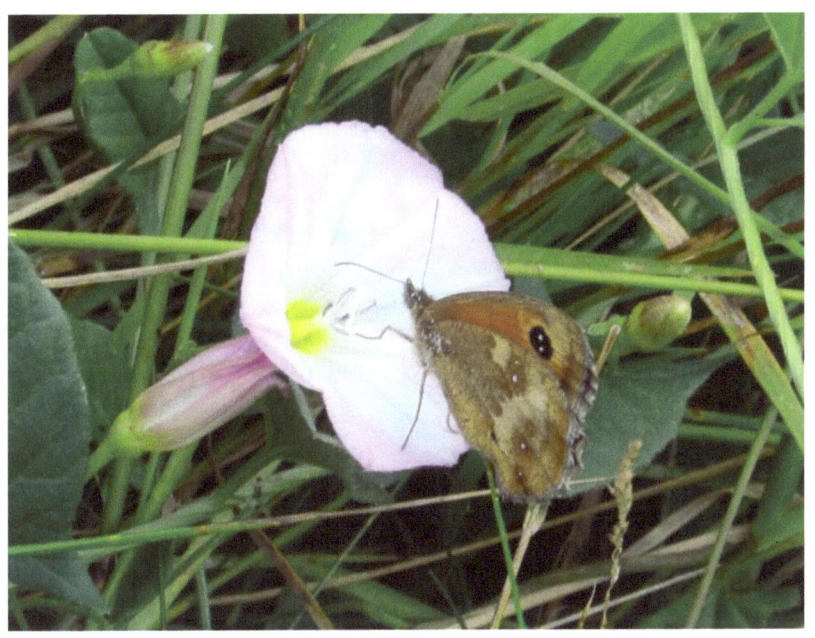

SMALL HEATH BUTTERFLY

This butterfly looks like a dead leaf which helps camouflage it. It's drinking nectar from a bindweed flower.

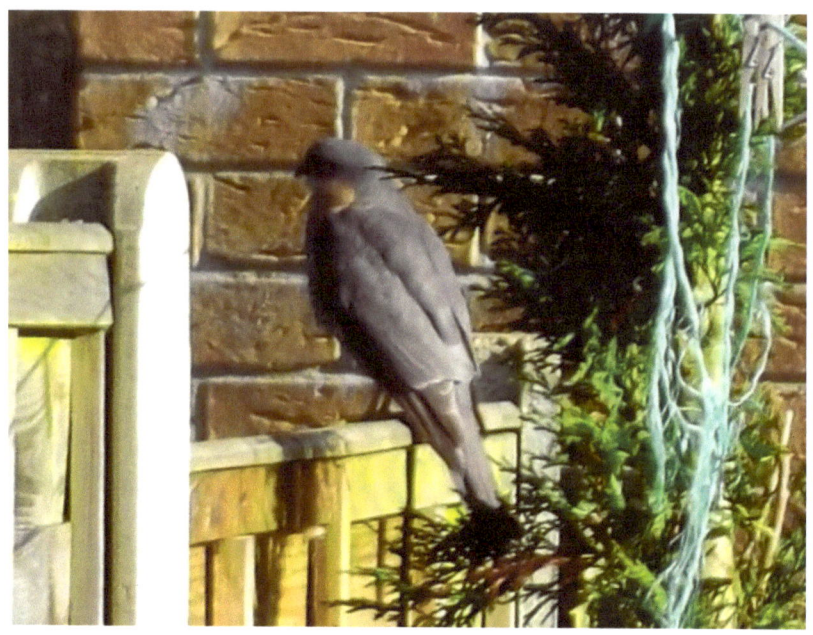

SPARROWHAWK

This is a rare visitor to the garden but can be seen in fields and edges of woods. It's a bird of prey and feeds on smaller birds like wrens, tits and finches.

The sparrowhawk has a high pitched call. It builds nests of twigs on branches near the trunks and has 4-5 eggs that are a very pretty light blue with brown speckles.

The sparrowhawk like all the hawks and birds of prey have very good eyesight and can spot their prey from high up in the sky.

Other birds of prey are Falcons, eagles, Kites, Harriers and buzzards.

When you are on a journey look up in the sky and you should see one hovering around looking for food.

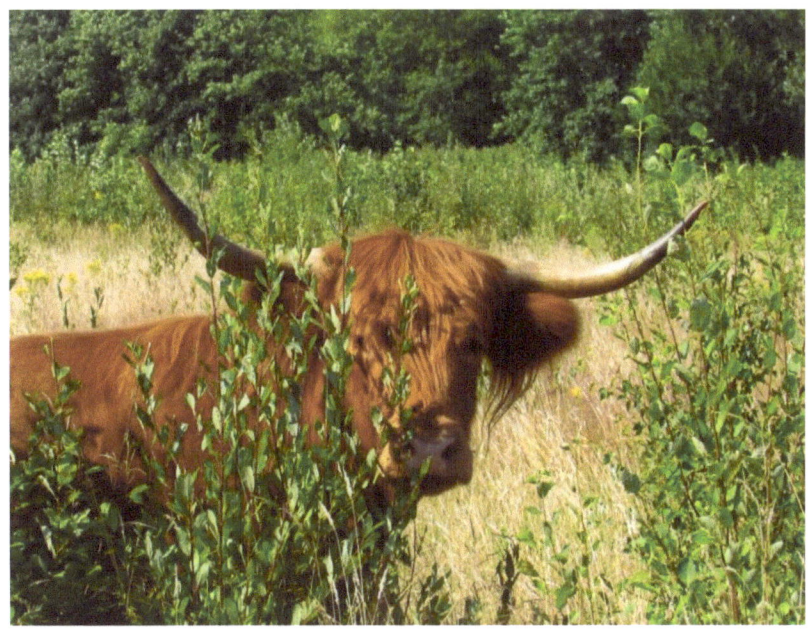

HIGHLAND COW

A real beastie although not wild as such they are found on nature reserves because they eat the grasses and stop the fields getting overgrown. Sometimes there are wild horses too.

THE END

Check out my other books on Amazon;

Children's books;
Bugz and other creepy crawleez.
How the unicorn became extinct and go-carts were
invented and other stories.
Lummy Lollops.
Rosa Villosa.
Teds in trouble and other rhyming tales.

Older children;
Faeries wear boots.
The caretaker.

Photo books;
Garden close-ups.
Magical Woodland.
Cornwall.

Poetry;
Mind.